THROUGH THE LE

VEHICLES OF
HOME GU/

Historic Military Press

Home Guard shoulder flash and county insignia. Both of these belonged to the commanding officer of the 28th (West Bromwich) Battalion, South Staffordshire, Home Guard.

MARTIN F. MACE

To find out about other titles produced by
Historic Military Press visit our website at www.historicmilitarypress.com.
Alternatively please write to us free of charge at
Customer Services, Historic Military Press,
Freepost SEA 11014, Pulborough, West Sussex, RH20 4BR,
or telephone our freephone number: 0800 071 7419.

HISTORIC MILITARY PRESS

VEHICLES OF THE HOME GUARD

First published 2001 by Historic Military Press,

ISBN 1-901313-08-05

All the photographs within this book, except where stated, have been produced by the kind permission of the Tank Museum at Bovington, from whose excellent collection they have been sourced. For the other illustrations my grateful thanks go to the following people: Mrs. Mary Taylor; Mr. E. Wilson; Peerage Books Limited; The Eastbourne Library; The Trustees of the Imperial War Museum; and the Trustees of Michelham Priory. The badges on page 1 are from the Historic Military Press Collection.

In compling this book I would like to thank the following individuals, in no particular order, without whom the project would have taken that much longer: Mr. Alan Wakefield, Curator Photograph Archive, Imperial War Museum; Mrs. Mary Taylor; Mrs. Helen Poole, Senior Museums Officer, Sussex Archaeological Society; Mr. Marcus Grehan; Mr. David Butt, Commerical Director, Tank Museum Bovington; Mr. Keith Downer. There is one person who needs particular mention and that is Mr. David Fletcher, Librarian of the Tank Musuem at Bovington. His generous donation of time and help has been invaluable in the creation of this book.

The following authors need mention for their excellent books: P. Crook (Sussex Home Guard, Middleton Press, 1998); Mr. David Carroll (The Home Guard, Sutton, 1999); S.P. Mackenzie, (The Home Guard, Oxford, 1996); Michael Sedgwick and Mark Giles (A-Z of cars of the 1930s, Bay View Books, 1993); Major Frederick Myatt MC (Modern Small Arms, Salamander, 1978); amongst others.

FRONT COVER: Men of the Littlehampton (Sussex) Home Guard motorbike section on parade with their mounts, Littlehampton, July 1940
(By kind permission of Mr. E. Wilson)

Printed in the United Kingdom by
Selsey Press Ltd, 84 High Street, Selsey, Chichester, West Sussex PO20 0QH
Telephone: 01243 605234 • Email: sales@selseypress.co.uk

HISTORIC MILITARY PRESS
Green Arbor, Rectory Road, Storrington, West Sussex, RH20 4EF. Telephone/Fax: 01903 741941

www.historicmilitarypress.com.

As the last of the small ships limped home packed with troops plucked from the bullet ridden sands of Dunkirk, the French hastily improvised a defence line on the Aisne and Somme rivers, praying that the Maginot Line to the east would hold. Within a week, German forces had reached the Marne, completely outflanking the Maginot Forts. Declared an open city, Paris fell without resistance. On the 22nd June 1940, its last vestiges of resistance having crumbled, France formally surrendered.

Britain now stood alone.

Men of the Rustington, West Sussex, LDV and their improvised transport, June 1940.
(By kind permission of Mrs. Mary Taylor.)

As it began to look increasingly likely that the might of the German war machine would arrive on British shores, Winston Churchill and his government harnessed the collective resolve of its citizens. At 9pm on Tuesday 14th May 1940 the Secretary of State for War, Anthony Eden, made his now immortal speech. In this broadcast he stated "..we want large numbers of such men, who are British subjects between the ages of 17 and 65, to come forward now and offer their services in order to make assurance doubly sure. The name of the new force that is to be raised will be the 'Local Defence Volunteers'..." The idea was to reinforce the weakened British army by a unit of unpaid volunteers that would become trained and equipped to deal with a German attack in their locality.

In the first few days after Eden's appeal about a quarter of a million men had come forward. As the Battle of Britain reached its peak at the end of the summer this had grown to over one million. In July 1940 as the LDV was receiving an ever-increasing volume of supplies and equipment, the name was changed. The Home Guard, immortalised by the BBC series 'Dad's Army', was born. As fighting units the early Home Guard Battalions were weak, their backbone often being those men whose medal ribbons proclaimed them to be First World War veterans. With the help of Regular or Territorial Army instructors, for a few hours each week, these volunteers were gradually welded into a more useful military force. With time came proper rifles, ammunition, military ranks and insignia, battledress uniforms and even, eventually, military vehicles. In many cases though, it was years before the latter reached a Home Guard unit - if at all. Until then, improvisation, the watchword of wartime Britain, was to be the order of the day. Some Battalions would manufacture their own vehicles, make requisitions of redundant military vehicles in a museum, or simply press into service whatever came to hand. Some of these vehicles were formidable weapons. Others, like the sight of the early LDV (consisting of men of all ages) attempting to drill, could hardly have reassured the onlookers.

'Vehicles of the Home Guard' is not intended to act as a complete reference source. Such a book would be nigh on impossible. It is hoped to provide both an interesting and informative glimpse of a part of the history of the LDV and Home Guard that has been all but ignored in most other publications.

To many of the people who read this book, some of the contraptions illustrated will do little but raise a smile. It is easy, with hindsight, to be cynical and scathing, but at the time the design, construction and use of these vehicles was a matter of national importance. They helped lift and maintain the national resolve. In a way they helped to support the message that Churchill once sent to the enemy on the nations behalf, saying "we shall fight on the beaches, we shall fight on the landing grounds, we shall fight in the fields and in the streets, we shall fight in the hills - we shall never surrender".

★ ★ ★ ★ ★

Some Home Guard units were lucky to obtain reasonable equipment comparatively soon after being established. More often than not though, this was a result of the generosity or ingenuity of individual members as opposed to rapid equipping on behalf of the War Office. This armoured car, **above**, was built for a battalion of the Maidenhead (Berkshire) Home Guard. Crude but effective, this rather rough-looking armoured car carries a Vickers machine gun in the turret, and has an aperture for a Bren gun or rifle beside the driver. This Home Guard

unit was lucky in having a local businessman, Colonel Tickler, at its head. Colonel Tickler was the owner of a well-known Berkshire fruit-preserving firm, and placed the staff and equipment at his factory at the service of his Home Guard section. Indeed, many of the male staff had emulated their boss and also enrolled in the Battalion. It must be pointed out that the female employees played their part in constructing such armoured cars, but were prevented from actually serving in the Home Guard. The War Office had decided from the outset that women would not be permitted to sign up in the LDV or Home Guard. It was not until 1943 that they were finally admitted as Auxiliaries, unable to wear uniforms or carry weapons. "Tickler's Army", as the unit became known, eventually produced several armoured cars. This example was built around the chassis of a 1935 Sunbeam 25hp saloon. Donations raised the £5 that was needed to buy the car. Once in the workshop, the original bodywork was removed and replaced by an armoured shell. This had been constructed from steel plates that, in the words of the original caption, were of the kind that could be found lying around in most factories. When the vehicle was shown to the local press, who christened it the 'Tickler Tank', it was noted that plans had been drawn up for a second version. This was to have two turrets from which four machine guns could provide a complete circle of fire. It is not recorded whether or not such a monstrosity was ever built!

brooms to the inspecting officer! The War Office desperately tried to keep abreast of the situation but was completely incapable of locating enough supplies in this country. A far from atypical company of the Home Guard in Caernarvonshire received the grand total of six Lee Enfield rifles. Not bad until one considers that this was for over 400 men! Emergency orders were placed across the Atlantic, and eventually some 100,000 mothballed Springfield and Remington rifles arrived from the United States. The rifle in the picture at first appears to be a British pattern 1913 rifle. However, it is in fact one of the hastily procured American rifles. With a .300" calibre, the Model '17 rifle had its origin in the First World War, and was in fact based on the British 1913 pattern rifle - hence the similarity in appearance. Whilst some units had to make do with 'knocked up' vehicles, others were more fortunate. The men of the Bristol Home Guard in the picture **below** maybe riding on a standard military design of armoured car manufactured by Thorneycroft in the inter-war years.

Taken about the same time as the previous photograph, the one **above** clearly illustrates the disparity in equipment between individual Home Guard units. It is the 29th August 1940 and the location is the village of West Farleigh, near Maidstone. Here the West Farleigh Platoon Commander, ex-Grenadier Guardsman 2nd Lieutenant J.W. Oxley, tries out their new armoured car. The scene is all too reminiscent of the BBC series 'Dads Army', with cloth caps and much improvisation. The vehicle is an old 30hp Buick presented to the unit by a local resident. Transformation to armoured car is achieved by simply welding or bolting steel plating over the windows and radiators. No machine guns are available, so slots are cut into the steel plating through which rifles and pistols could be pointed. One interesting point in this photograph is the rifle held by Oxley. From the outset, and for many months, the Home Guard was desperately short of equipment. Not without reason were detachments of the LDV seen on parade presenting spades and

Above: Could this be one of the first ventures into the world of military vehicles by a company that was eventually to become one of Britain's leading tank manufacturers? Founded in 1919 Alvis soon developed a reputation for building pioneering sports cars, particularly with the introduction of front wheel drive. In the 1930's the company drifted away from the manufacture of overt sports cars to the introduction of more luxurious models. In this, Alvis was intending to challenge its rivals such as Bentley. From then on Alvis devoted itself to the design and construction of tanks and other armoured vehicles. The rather crude steel plates added here disguise a vehicle belonging to the Kings Lynn Home Guard, Norfolk. That only the front two seats and the radiator front have been protected suggests that this is one of the earliest attempts at adapting a civilian vehicle for use by the Home Guard. It is likely that the source car was an Alvis Silver Eagle, of which 1161 were built up to 1933.

Below: Both the vehicle and the Home Guard here are from the Luton Home Guard, wherein lies a clue as to the manufacturer of the source vehicle.

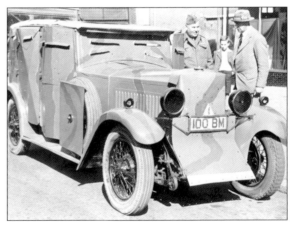

Luton was, and still is, home to one of Britain's most famous marques - Vauxhall. The car is a Vauxhall 20/60 saloon, one of the first of the GM inspired Vauxhalls.

The local adaptation shown **right** has a most interesting basis, one that was no doubt the gift of a wealthy local beneficiary. The source vehicle is thought to be a 2.5 litre Jaguar 4 door saloon. This vehicle was the first of the overhead valve designs from the firm SS - Jaguar was just the model name. In the 1930s Jaguar was the name applied to its products by the motor manufacturer SS. Based in Blackpool, it was not until 1945 that the firm changed its name to bring it in line with its products. The 2.5 litre is described as an excellent machine - its bodywork elegant and comfortable, the engine smooth and flexible. No doubt such characteristics evaporated by the time the Home Guard had finished! Photographed by the Western Morning News in Exeter, this armoured car belonged to the Camelford Home Guard. It is attracting much attention as it participates in the Camelford War Weapons Week procession. Note the Bren gun mounted on the top, and 'HG' painted on the left-hand side of the windscreen. One wonders what has become of FXP 478 in the years since the war? Shown **below**, and not from quite the same breeding, is this armoured car belonging to the Blackburn (Lancashire) Home Guard. Described as an Austin Riley (Austin chassis, Riley bodywork?) type, it was photographed on the 30th September 1940. This vehicle has undergone the most basic of conversions, with very little armour plating added. Even the windows have remained, though now coated in camouflage paint. The interesting feature here is the

gun mounted in the back. It is a 1918 A2 Browning Automatic Rifle. Like the Model '17 described on page 5, these rifles were part of the emergency supplies purchased by the War Office from the United States. In spite of its somewhat uneasy position, which made it rather heavy for a rifle and rather light for a machine gun, several thousand were shipped to the UK for supply to the Home Guard. Its introduction was not without problems - its .30" calibre caused the Quartermaster General's department many a headache. First used in action on the 13th September 1918, the Browning remained in service in the United States for many years, undergoing few changes.

No sooner had Eden's broadcast finished than the cynics and critics started to make themselves heard. Even the title LDV did not escape. A few interpreted these initials as standing for 'Look, Duck and Vanish'! To the men of the Home Guard, and the majority of the British people, their presence had a real purpose. There can be no doubt that the existence of such a national organisation drawn from the ranks of the ordinary population had a positive effect on the country's morale in those difficult times. Here men of the Littlehampton (Sussex) Home Guard parade their motorbike units on the sports ground of St. Nicholas' School, Granville Road, Littlehampton. The photograph is owned by Mr. Ernest Wilson who is pictured sitting on the motorbike on the far right - with goggles on his head. Known as 'Tug' to the rest of the unit, Ernest was the despatch rider for its commanding officer, Colonel Cowie. He can still remember much of his work in the Home Guard. "When on duty we used to sleep in the club house, ready for action. One night there was an air raid over the town and a house in New Road was hit by bombs. One of the occupants, a woman, was killed. The rifles were also delivered to the clubhouse, though completely caked in grease. Someone fired one by accident, shooting a hole in the wooden floor of the building!" In this picture the motorbike riders have these rifles, the ubiquitous American Model '17 imports, slung across their backs. Also worthy of note is the combination of titles mounted on the handlebars. The fact that both the names Home Guard and LDV are used would suggest that this picture was taken sometime in July 1940. After the excitement of the early months had passed, many members of the Home Guard began to find the continuous night-time and weekend duties a considerable burden on their lives. Absenteeism grew and there was no real disciplinary mechanism for dealing with such occurrences. In fact this situation remained unaltered until November 1941 when proper military ranks, discipline and procedures were introduced. From this point on, members of the Home Guard could be prosecuted if they failed to carry out duties or regular training. Clarification of exactly what was expected was also made - a maximum of 48 hours a month being specified. To ease the enforcement of this new rule, men were allowed to resign before it came into force.

Rapid response Home Guard style! These two remarkable adaptations are both private designs based on the same vehicle - the Fordson Major tractor. The picture **above** shows the 1st style, whilst in the other is an example of the 2nd style. Even though these armoured tractors may not have proved particularly fast, the quality of build and thickness of steel plate used is quite impressive. The turrets also appear intricate and well armed. On the downside, perhaps the most obvious drawback, other than speed, is space. There does not appear to be enough room even for the driver, let alone any gunners or stores. However, the biggest contradiction lies not with the actual vehicle, but with the designer. Both the 1st and 2nd styles were designed by Leo Villa, who as many motoring historians will recall was the mechanic and friend of Sir Malcolm Campbell. Both were men who steadfastly pursued the quest for speed and ultimately the world land speed record. That they should be behind one of the slowest vehicles supplied to the Home Guard will no doubt bring a smile to many! In his 'Book of the Racing Campbells' Richard Hough describes the extremely close relationship between the two men. Indeed Leo

Villa had a special place in the Campbell household. In the photograph of the 1st style, Leo Villa can be seen admiring his work - or perhaps he is pondering the question of how the driver, having successfully squeezed himself behind the steering wheel, will be able to see over the radiator protection!

The story of Sir Malcolm Campbell begins before the First World War, when as a young man he purchased a huge Darracq car, painted it blue, christened it 'Bluebird' and took it racing at Brooklands. It was as fast as it was dangerous. There then followed the superb aero-engined Sunbeam which, following a series of extraordinary escapes and misfortunes, succeeded in taking the ultimate land speed record for the first time. It is known that Villa and Campbell worked together on other projects for the Home Guard. As well as using the Fordson Major as a basis for their designs, they also developed armoured bodies for a number of Dodge vehicles. Leo Villa is trying a light machine gun out for size, whilst Sir Malcolm Campbell takes the wheel. Whilst Leo Villa was the main inspiration behind the Fordson conversions, it was Campbell who developed the Dodges. In the example **below-left** he had the top part of the armoured shell cut off. Inside was then mounted a complete short six-pounder, including pedestal stand and shield. This gun and mounting would have originally been fitted to a First World War Male Tank - as can be seen **bottom-right**. Now strictly a self-propelled gun as opposed to an armoured car, this vehicle was christened 'Tubby the Tank Buster'. It was operated by the Somerford section of the Christchurch (then Hampshire but now Dorset) Home Guard.

As will be seen throughout this book, production of many of the LDV and Home Guard's vehicles, (in particular the earlier adaptations), was based on standard civilian motor cars. One of the more productive, and therefore photographed, suppliers was the Berkshire jam producing company belonging to Colonel Tickler of the Maidenhead (Berkshire) Home Guard. In these two photographs we can see a before and after of armoured car production. Having purchased or been donated a suitable base vehicle, the first step often involves the removal of most of the original bodywork, though this only happened when a completely new armoured shell was to be made. In the **top** photo, a mechanic stands back to admire his work. Here a Sunbeam 25hp chassis

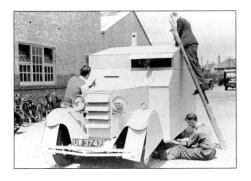

stands somewhat naked, despite the addition of a new steel and aluminum frame. The lack of most of the original features means that it is almost impossible to identify the actual model. Sunbeam was a British manufacturer that had its heyday in the 1920s. It had been founded in 1895, with its first car completed during 1901. In the twenties it was producing successful racing cars and record-breakers, as well excellent production touring and sports models. The early 1930s saw models being made that rivalled the best from the competition - in particular Bentley and Alvis. A gentleman called Rootes purchased Sunbeam in 1935, and from there on the company was called Sunbeam-Talbot. The completely un-aerodynamic design below may well represent the re-incarnated Sunbeam, though the caption does not provide us with much detail, except to say that this is the same factory. Workmen provide the finishing touches to this armoured-van - for want of a better expression. By comparing this vehicle to other Tickler designs, it appears that this might be one of the earliest attempts. The fact that the machine gun position is forward facing gives a very limited field of fire, and the driver has the smallest possible viewing slip does little to add to performance. There is one interesting feature - the periscope mounted on top of the rear body.

Having completed the armoured-van on the previous page, the staff at Tickler's were apparently unhappy with the result. This armoured car is built on the same chassis - that belonging to UW 3746. This version is certainly more armoured-car like in appearance. There are several other fundamental improvements: improved drivers' visibility, a co-drivers position and, most importantly, a revolving turret for the Vickers machine gun. Despite the fact that the original caption states otherwise, it would be most unlikely that the obviously thin plating used on the sides and back would stop penetration by small arms and rifle fire. With time, some Home Guard units would become remarkably well equipped - as is

the case in this lineup of vehicles from the Kings Lynn (Norfolk) Battalion. The line up includes a 1934 Alvis; one 1934 and two 1935 Hillmans; a Railton; a 1934 Rover; two Fords and a sprinkling of motorbikes. One of the most interesting vehicles in the group is that third from left. This vehicle is the only one not provided with the anti-grenade netting, armour plating and indeed any armament. This suggests that this vehicle is a staff car, no doubt for the Commanding Officer of the unit, as opposed to an armoured or other fighting vehicle. The same group, including the armoured car 'Freda', can also be seen **below**, though this time photographed in a different location.

In the early days of the LDV and Home Guard there was absolutely no co-ordination or control over production of its armoured cars and vehicles. This was the time when 'Dad's Army' was at its best. However, with the militarisation of the Home Guard throughout the summer of 1940, steps were made to introduce standardised designs and vehicles. Some, such as the Beaverette (page 31) were production designs, whilst others, though from a common idea or directive, might still be produced at a local level. One of the most interesting designs from the latter group was the 'Bison'. The basic concept and design of these vehicles was proposed by the Concrete Company Limited. Whether an example of patriotic inspiration or astute marketing, their idea was remarkably simple and effective. They had, basically,

taken a 6x4 or 6x2 truck chassis and turned it into a mobile concrete pillbox. By this point of the war, the British countryside was becoming laced by a network of inter-linking defence lines. One of the principle features of these stop-lines were defensive structures constructed from concrete and steel. Called pillboxes, these bunkers would house infantry or anti-tank units providing valuable cover from enemy fire. Someone at the Concrete Company Limited, realising the potential of these buildings, decided to take the theory one stage further and make them mobile! Produced almost entirely for the use of the Home Guard, several hundred of these vehicles finally saw service. A small fraction of this production run is shown **below**, awaiting delivery at one of the factories of the Concrete Company Limited.

The bison was certainly unsophisticated to say the least. There were basically two designs. The first consisted of separate concrete cab and rear pillboxes, whilst in the second type the Bison was produced as a single unit. Consisting of a thick layer of concrete there is no doubt that it would have been immune from small arms fire, and possibly even a light field gun. Many of the type were used for airfield defence, operated either by Home Guard units or, in some cases, by men from the Royal Air Force Regiment.

The Bison shown in this picture is on airfield defence duty at an unknown airfield in Western Command. We know this is a military airfield by the presence of the twin-engined aircraft in the background. This medium range bomber is an American built Douglas A-20 Havoc, given the designation of Douglas Boston by the British. Just as interesting is the aircraft taxiing past the front of the Bison. This is believed to be a civilian operated De Havilland Albatross from the fleet of West Coast Air Services Ltd. It is thought that this airline operated from

Bristol airport, carrying out scheduled wartime mail and passenger services to both the Scilly Isles and the Republic of Ireland. In his wartime diaries Wing Commander Hal Randall DFC recalls the time he encountered one of these passenger aircraft during a RAF Coastal Command patrol. "On the 15th April 1942 I was on a convoy escort to a cable laying ship off the South Coast of Eire. To our amazement we suddenly saw a four-engined German Condor bomber approaching from the west, apparently about to attack the ships. I mentally crossed myself, and banked our Blenheim round in a steep turn so that we could get into an attacking position. Sweeping out of the sun I opened fire on the 'attacker'. Luckily my shooting was poor, for as I came round on the quarter attack we saw that the Condor had twin fins! It was a British aircraft that we had just attacked. It was an Albatross, a very rare aircraft, that was on a daily flight from Shannon!" Another Bison appears to be resting on the tarmac on the other side of this aircraft, though judging by the presence of the bricks blocking the wheels both are on static duty as opposed to a mobile patrol.

Despite the number of these vehicles that were built few survive - no doubt a result of their pitiful road speed and handling. Trying to stop a truck fitted out with a couple of tons of concrete pillbox strapped to its back would have been no mean feat! It is believed that one example was on show at the Headquarters of the Royal Air Force Regiment at Catterick. There is also a replica on show at the Tank Museum at Bovington, clearly showing the separate concrete cab. The pressure on its Thorneycroft chassis must be truly immense! The Bison idea would eventually

skywards from the top edges! This must truly be one of the most ungainly motor vehicles to see the light of day. Access was gained by climbing the metal stepladder set into the concrete on the right hand side. Once inside, the next challenge for the driver was actually being able to see where he or she was going. In this case it appears that the poor victim is straining to get a view of the road in front!

The caption for this vehicle states that the concrete was proof against small arms and armour-piercing

be produced on any available donor commercial vehicle. The example **above** illustrates a more compact vehicle. This picture has been touched up, either by the sensor or by the organisation that intended to use it. Other pictures in the same series show that the concrete construction had not been completed, with reinforcing rods still poking

rounds. The crew it required was between six and ten men. Their biggest challenge though must have been to prevent the engine from overheating. Making the engine drag around that weight and then only creating a couple of thin slits for the radiator must surely have been a recipe for disaster!

A similar development like the Bison programme was the Armadillo series. As with the Bison this involved the use of any available commercial truck, though in these cases the original cabs were retained and a different, non-concrete, fighting section employed. The Armadillo (**above and below**) was used to equip both the Home Guard and the RAF airfield defence units. The Armadillo was normally armed with a Lewis machine gun, whilst firing slits were provided in the sides, front and rear for riflemen. The driver was not forgotten, for the cab was usually armoured with mild steel.

The basis of the Armadillo series was the wooden defensive rear structure. Built with greater ease and increased speed, these wooden boxes replaced the heavier and more complicated concrete pillboxes of the Bisons. The first stage was the construction of the outer wooden frame, followed by a smaller interior that fitted inside. The space between this double skin would then be filled up with pebbles and gravel.

In the **top** picture carpenters are busy constructing the double skins. Note how the firing slits are bridged between both walls. Once the woodwork was completed they were bolted to the flat bed on the lorry using a crane - as can be seen in the photograph on the **left**.

By adopting this method of construction the build time for individual Armadillos was far less than that for the Bison. Trials were also to show that these structures offered its occupants complete protection against small arms fire. In effect, they would serve more as a mobile rifle post than as a pillbox like the Bison.

In this picture on the **left** the wooden box is being filled with gravel and pebbles from an overhead hopper. This United commercial has yet to be camouflaged, but does carry white blackout markings (as can be seen on the bumper and running boards) and the light shades. Once this stage was completed, the vehicle would be taken to the paint shop for the last bits of work to be completed.

This final work, and the mass production of the Armadillos, can be seen in the picture **below**. The line of vehicles on the left are having the camouflage paintwork applied, whilst those on the right are having the mild steel plates added to the cabs. The size of the workshop, and the design of its construction, suggests that this is a railway depot. What is also of interest in this picture is the variety of different commercial manufacturers that are represented.

issued becoming the principle light machine-gun of the Home Guard. Spare magazine drums were mounted on the Armadillo walls, two for each gun. A rack was provided for three rifles, with spare ammunition in two boxes bolted to the floor. The final weapon included in the inventory was a flare gun - which can be seen in a wall-mounted holder on the left hand side of the Armadillo. The box fixed to the floor just below this contains the spare flares. The Armadillo finally developed into an armoured-metal shell, pre-dominantly fitted to standard military trucks. The original caption for the picture below states 'the inside of a Bison'. However, we know that because there is not an inch of concrete anywhere in sight, this is not the case. This is more likely to be the interior of the all-metal Armadillo units. In the side windows, equipped with sliding shutters, the sheer thickness of the metal armour is all too clear. Features typical of military vehicles of this period can also be seen - the canvas covered cushion on the centre bench; the fire extinguisher bolted to the floor; and the enormous spare wheel, carried inside for its protection.

The Armadillo, when fully equipped, carried a formidable array of weapons. In the view **above** we are looking down into the inside of an Armadillo unit. As the series was developed, military versions were developed for use predominantly by the regular army and airforce. However, as the war progressed these would also be released to the Home Guard, replaced in service by more conventional armoured vehicles. This Armadillo box was fitted to a 30cwt Bedford OY truck, and given the military designation Mark II mobile machine-gun post! In effect it was a 3 ton 4x2 mobile blockhouse! The Armadillo box was fitted on the rear of these standard 3-tonners, with the windscreen and radiator protected by light armour plating. Whilst there are only two shown, this vehicle had a compliment of three Lewis machine-guns. There are four mountings present, three on the sides and one for anti-aircraft fire. Although the Lewis gun, designed in 1910, had ceased to be the official light machine-gun of the British Infantry before 1939, many thousands were still held in store when the war started. In view of the desperate shortage of arms of all types, these were quickly re-

This photograph is a graphic illustration of Britain's vital industries at war. The large factory in the background is in fact the works of Morris Motors. (Note the camouflage paint that has been applied to the factory sheds and the huge surface air-raid shelter in the open ground just behind the armoured car). At one time Morris Motors had been the maker of nearly half of Britain's motor cars, despite having only started out producing bicycles. Correspondingly, its value to the wartime economy was immense. Like many large companies Morris started its own defence force. Indeed, it is one of their armoured cars that is shown here. However, Morris seems to have chosen not to affiliate its defence unit with the Home Guard and instead retain an independent force. This can be seen most clearly in the insert. Here the machine-gunner is wearing a uniform similar to that used by Fire Brigades of the time. His haversack is of a type issued to the ARP (Air Raid Precaution) service. His helmet, which carries a rolled up neck protector of oiled canvas and intended to protect against corrosives such as mustard gas, is from the same source. Interestingly, his only identification is the collar tabs and the buttons on his epaulettes. The former has the wording 'M.M. Ltd' - Morris Motors

Ltd. From the evidence in this photograph one would assume that Morris Motors was trying to achieve a combination of both the ARP and the Home Guard services. However, such a split personality may well have proved to be the units undoing. A close inspection of the 'machine-gun' mounted in the turret shows that it is in fact a wooden replica. It is possible that neither the ARP service nor the Home Guard were happy to fully support a unit that also fell under the influence of another department!

Above: Whatever critics may say about the LDV and Home Guard, what they lacked in skill and equipment was more than made up for in enthusiasm. In these two pictures soldiers from the Home Guard readily pose for press photographers. This curvaceous (!) armoured car belongs to the Cheadle Heath (Cheshire) Home Guard. It is another example of community involvement. The vehicle was built at a local factory, using a car and steel plates donated by others. The caption tells us that this vehicle, based on a 4x2 saloon, cost the grand total of £80. Its armoured body is claimed to be proof against machine gun and rifle fire. A revolving turret is fitted, though the Lewis or Vickers machine gun with which it is to be equipped is yet to arrive, despite the fact that this appears to be a quite well equipped unit. A pair of large double doors has been fitted at the back, allowing the armoured car to act as an ambulance if necessary. **Right:** Another ordinary saloon that has been adapted, again by the Maidenhead Home Guard, in the Tickler's jam factory. As well as adding radiator and windscreen protection, all the other windows have been removed and replaced by armoured plate. Slits have been cut into these for rifles - a total of 7 of which can protrude from this 'porcupine' at any one time. These are supported by a Vickers machine gun mounted through the roof. The reporter in this case had added a stirring caption for the wartime British population: "The factories of England are prepared for all emergencies, but are still carrying on with their work, despite the attempts by Nazi raiders to stop them. This famous preserving factory in Berkshire has its own Home Guard, and they post lookouts on the roof during air raids!"

poster. American Model '17 rifles protrude from the windows, whilst a Vickers machine gun points skywards. The mascot mounted proudly on the radiator provides the clue as to the car's original maker - the American company Hudson.

The only disparity with the original caption relates to the exact model. The wartime press photographer has listed this as a Terraplane. However, a close study of the catalogues for this firm suggest that this vehicle may well be a Hudson Six. Approximately 9,000 of these 4-door sedans were built in 1935. Interesting design features include umbrella handle handbrakes, narrow grilles and steel-spoke wheels. The standard British package included rear bumpers, which can just be seen on the picture on the previous page. One downside was the fact that the electrics still remained six-volt for the British market. Hudson can trace its origin back to Thomas-Detroit, which was started in 1906. It produced its first car in 1906, and was named Hudson after the Detroit tycoon who owned the largest department store in the world. With time the cars established a reputation for having sprightly performance and strong build. The Hudsons imported into the UK, as no doubt this was one, were assembled from kits in Chiswick often using British built bodies.

Over the next couple of pages are a few pictures illustrating further vehicles produced by the Maidenhead Home Guard - see page 4. Under the directorship of Colonel Tickler, whose staff and factory were used to carry out the conversions, a large number of vehicles were eventually manufactured for the Home Guard. The picture **above** is quite impressive, and indeed would have made an ideal image for a Home Guard recruitment

The armour mounted on this radiator is quite unique, though one wonders what it did to the cooling airflow! The vehicle that has been used in this conversion is another with American influence, though built in Britain. Despite the fact that the 1930s presented a move away from the influence of its mother company, Ford of Britain still produced models with a distinct American influence. Many feel that this is certainly the case with this model - the V8-78. Fitted with a Lincoln-Zephyr style vee grille, insect like recessed headlamps, a vee screen and a bonnet that opened both upwards and sideways, this vehicle saw 4331 examples roll off the production lines in 1937. No doubt the almost unique headlamps on this V8 saloon presented a slight problem when it came to obeying the blackout regulations. Unable to find headlamp shades that would fit, the Home Guard had to resort to painting the lights out completely with black paint. As no replacement lights seem to have been fitted, this would make use of this vehicle at night a pretty daunting (and unpleasant) proposition! In an effort to provide as much protection as possible, (or were they anticipating the occasional nocturnal prang!), Colonel Tickler devised a cheap and effective way of upgrading the radiator and windscreen protection. Both were fitted with a 9" wide container that had a

cavity in the middle. This was then filled with gravel and pebbles - as can be seen in the photograph **above** where a member of the Home Guard fills the radiator protection. Tests were carried out on the devices, and it was found that all of the bullets fired at them failed to penetrate both sides of the container and the gravel contents (**see insert**). A test control of steel sheeting, tested at the same time, was cleanly pierced. Also of interest in the top picture is the weapon that the sergeant is holding.

For the enthusiast we can tell you that this appears to be a Luger Parabellum Artillery Modell 08. Fitted with the characteristic 'snail' drum magazine (holding 32 9mm rounds) and wooden butt, this is now an extremely rare piece - and was almost as uncommon when this picture was taken on the 30th August 1940. In a sense this gun was the forerunner of the submachine gun, and served the German Army with distinction in the First World War. Herein lies another example of improvisation symptomatic of the Home Guard. This weapon was unlikely to have been issued by the British military authorities. Was it 'liberated' from a local museum, or a souvenir of service in an earlier war put back into use against its origin owners?

A typical view of wartime London (**top**). The Home Guard operate a sandbagged rifle post outside an important building; on the wall behind them is pinned a sign stating "this is not a public shelter - the nearest is at Stangate opposite St. Thomas's Hospital"; to the left a poster promotes child health. The men pointing their rifles at the camera (no slip of the trigger finger please) are from the London County Council (LCC) Battalion, Home Guard. The building they are guarding is in fact their place of work - County Hall. Pictured whilst on patrol on the 23rd August 1940, this vehicle was the first of a number of armoured cars that were to be built for the Battalion. The vehicle was almost certainly one of the fleet of vehicles used for official duties. The caption suggests that the armoured car was based on a Rolls-Royce, and indeed it is running on wheels that are characteristic of the Rolls-Royce marque. A badge, shaped like a pair of wings, can be seen on the lower edge of the steel shell but, despite the closet examination, does not provide any clues. The whole vehicle appears to be of substantial build, with much attention to detail - note the small side viewing hatch for the driver; the small access panel on the engine cowling; and even the pennant flying from the front! Carrying a Vickers machine gun mounted in the revolving turret, the armoured car required a crew of

three. This comprised of the driver, a gunner and the observer. As well as assisting the gunner, the observer was also armed with a standard service rifle. Records show that this vehicle was built in the council's own workshops. **Above:** Looking like something out of 'Star Wars' this is another of the LCC Battalion armoured cars. It is shown here entering the area of County Hall. The design of this example, that had the registration CP 50, is very similar to the vehicle above. Indeed this is also thought to have been a Rolls-Royce limousine from the official fleet. Basing an armoured car on such a large and strong chassis has an obvious advantage in terms of space - note the hand and face peering out of the back of the vehicle!

Above: Winston Churchill and General Wade Haynes (standing just behind Churchill) inspect an armoured car of the American Troop Home Guard, July 1940. Known to its members as the American Mechanised Defence Corps, this unit of the Home Guard was established by Mr. A.P. Buquor, a member of the American Embassy Staff in London. As well as from the staff of the embassy, members were drawn from all parts of the American ex-pat community in Britain. Based in London the Unit equipped itself entirely at its own expense, eventually possessing items still unavailable to much of the rest of the Home Guard. This included light and heavy machine guns, sub-machine guns, hand-grenades and a number of vehicles. The armoured car shown here is obviously well designed and constructed. Built on an American chassis and equipped with items such as a periscope, (see the left-hand side of the windscreen panel), and sealed door it maybe that this vehicle was imported complete from the United States. For that reason it may well be an example of a commercial design produced in America at the time.

Throughout the history of the Home Guard can be seen acts of individual generosity. The picture **right** represents just one more example. Beneath all the

plates of steel is, believe it or not, a Bentley saloon. In fact the source car is so well hidden that we are completely unable to establish what model from this luxurious marque was used. Mrs. J. Appleton presented this car to the 3rd (Stevenage) Battalion of the Hertfordshire Home Guard in August 1940.

Pictured on the 2nd of that month is Mr. J. Appleton (standing at right) who at the time was the managing director of a local Stevenage company - E.S.A. This couple had the car converted at their own expense before making the presentation. As ever, ingenuity was the order of the day - note the Lewis gun sat on a mounting removed from a redundant open cockpit RAF aircraft!

Above: Men of the Yorkshire Home Guard ambushing their armoured car during exercises in the Yorkshire Dales. The caption for this picture suggests that the chassis on which this vehicle was built came from a Sunbeam saloon car. Home Guard training exercises often present an almost comical image when viewed from photographs such as this - an image all too apparent from the BBC series 'Dad's Army'. However, the risks were real, compounded by the fact that many of the Home Guard were nothing more than part-time soldiers. In this picture one can see a Molotov cocktail exploding in the road behind the armoured car. A few seconds earlier and this could have dropped onto the canvas roof of the armoured car, burning through to the occupants inside. The resulting carnage is best left to the imagination! Tony Renoir still recalls an incident that occurred during his time as a member of the Worthing (Sussex) Home Guard. "We often went upto Cissbury Ring where the regular army had established a complete training centre. This included a range for practising hand grenade throwing. Now, I was never very good at cricket - I just couldn't throw a ball. There we were in the trench when it was my turn. I pulled out the pin and began to swing my arm in an effort to lob the grenade as far as possible. However my hand bashed against the back wall of the trench and I dropped the grenade! Fortunately the Company Commander, Colonel Coleman, was standing right behind me. He grabbed the grenade, hurling it away so that it exploded in midair. Naturally the moments that followed contained a number of distinctly un-military expressions!" In the picture **below** men of the Rustington (Sussex) Home Guard are about to depart for a days training. This Austin 10/4 saloon looks particularly overloaded and, with its 93" wheelbase described in the company literature as 'compact', not completely suited to being a Home Guard transport. One wonders how many ruts in the road would be passed before the trailer was rid of its human load!

(By kind permission of Mrs. M. Taylor)

Above: August 1940, and the Home Guard is on the move. This small convoy is from the 7th Battalion (Stroud) Gloucestershire Home Guard. The convoy consists of two armoured cars (seen in better detail below) and an ambulance. The 7th Battalion was fortunate in having a number of generous beneficiaries. Two local residents who donated the vehicles used to build the armoured cars provided the first acquisitions. Named 'Daniel' and 'The Eagle' both of these armoured cars are believed to have been built on the chassis taken from a Morris Cowley. Described as pedestrian but dependable, some 184,906 examples of this car were built between 1927 and 1930. It was available in a wide variety of styles, including tourer, saloon, and commercials. Using sheet steel of the approved thickness a local engineering firm then replaced the original bodywork with armoured shells. A number of other local tradesmen, as well as skilled members of the unit, also assisted. For all this work no charge was made. Finishing touches included the addition of camouflage paintwork, a pair of Hotchkiss machine guns, wing mounted markers to assist the driver's steering and visibility and even rear view mirrors mounted on top of the armoured body. The third and final vehicle was donated soon after the completion of the armoured cars, and was immediately turned into an ambulance. In the top picture it is quite clear that this ambulance had been a hearse in its previous occupation! Note the two elderly Home Guard leaning on the rear door - could they be hedging their bets by choosing to be carried around in this vehicle? Perhaps it was a sign of the feelings of the nation at the time, but the acquisition and transformation of all three vehicles only cost the unit 30/-, and this was for a single particular item that had to be paid for!

It is amongst the specialist units of the Home Guard that we can find some of the more interesting vehicles and methods of transport. The London Passenger Transport Board Home Guard is one such example. Formed from the management, drivers, conductors and mechanics from a number of the wartime London bus depots this unit, somewhat naturally, decided to make use of one of the vehicles that it had most readily available - a bus! What was once an AEC Regent double-decker now serves as an enormous armoured personnel carrier (**above**). One can only guess at how horrendous such a vehicle would have been to drive! With such a limited turning circle, and almost no visibility for the driver it must surely have presented more of a danger to the architecture of London than it did to the enemy! In the view **right**, the sheer scale of the steel plating is all too obvious, as is the relatively high level of construction. Access would have been through the rear doors, with firing slits supplied for about ten riflemen.

London Transport eventually formed seven Home Guard battalions, serving under such exotic names

as the 'Camberwell Tram Depot Home Guard' or the 'Dartford Country Bus Depot Home Guard'.

Four wheels was not always the prerequisite of a Home Guard transport, as this picture of men from the Port of London Authority Home Guard shows. The location is the West India Docks, and the date is October 1941. The ranks of this Home Guard unit were drawn from amongst the employees of the Port of London, men who by their very nature had an intimate knowledge of this stretch of the River Thames. Nearly as sedate as the transport barge **above** is the patrol boat employed by the Birmingham Home Guard (**below**). This motor patrol boat was used on observation duties along the canal network of the Ladywood district of Birmingham - one of Britain's wartime industrial heartlands. Water based units were relatively common, and other well known examples include the Upper Thames Patrol (UTP). Within days of Anthony Eden's speech Sir Ralph Glyn, the MP for Abingdon, wrote to the War Office requesting permission to establish a waterborne unit of the LDV. The result was the creation of the UTP. This unit of experienced sailors covered a stretch of the Thames between Lechlade in Gloucestershire and Teddington in Middlesex. Each patrol covered 16 miles of river, with a 'stretch-commander' in charge. Formed at the same time as the UTP was the Trent River Patrol Home Guard. Again it was the same kind of recruit for the same kind of task, just a different stretch of river - the River Trent from Sawley to the Humber estuary. Sadly the Trent River Patrol suffered a number of fatalities among its members. Two men were accidentally shot during firing practice, and another pair drowned whilst on a patrol. Perhaps the most famous waterborne unit was the 9th Westmorland Battalion Home Guard. Its men, making use of fast speedboats armed with Vickers machine-guns, were tasked to patrol the open waters of Lake Windermere. Numbering over 100 men at its peak, this unit had been formed to relieve the men of the regular Army's inland waterways section, who had previously been the guardians of this stretch of water.

advantage that the Molotov possessed was its ridiculously simple method of construction. The Molotov is in effect a simple petrol bomb. Individual Home Guard units made them in their thousands from a pint bottle containing petrol, tar, creosote or any liquid that would burn. The fuse was a piece of petrol-soaked rag protruding from the neck of the bottle. Often the sides of the bottle would be scored with a glass-cutter in an effort to aid fragmentation. To use the Molotov cocktail,

As was usually the case at the beginning of the LDV (and Home Guard), improvisation was the order of the day. This photograph provides us with an ideal illustration. (Whilst the background is provided by another view of the Sunbeam based armoured car built for the Maidenhead Home Guard, (see page 4), it is the contraption in the foreground that is of as much interest.) This device is in fact a 'Molotov-slinger'. Named after the then Soviet Foreign Minister, the Molotov cocktail was basically the only anti-tank weapon that the LDV possessed in its early days. The device had first been used in the Spanish Civil War and then again in the Soviet-Finnish War - it was in the later conflict that the term Molotov cocktail first came into being. In the 'Local Defence Volunteers Instruction No.8 - 1940', the following reference was made regarding the use of Molotov cocktails: "From the moment that enemy tanks are located they must be harried, hunted, sniped and ambushed without respite until they are destroyed. Goliath was slain by David's sling, and the lessons of Spain and Finland confirm that tanks can be destroyed by men who have bravery, resource and determination to do so". As well as being of some value in the field, the other singular

one would have selected a target, lit the fuse and then thrown the bottle - hoping for the best. On hitting the enemy tank, (if the thrower was lucky), the bottle would shatter spilling the flammable liquid. As this flowed away the burning rag fuse would ignite it. The manuals were quite specific - the Molotov would be aimed at the vulnerable points such as engine compartments and air intakes. Molotov cocktails were usually made in batches, stacked in bottle crates and placed ready-at-hand in strategic locations. During this storage the bottles would be sealed to prevent evaporation of the petrol. How accurate could the attacker be using the Molotov-slinger was thankfully never put to the test! This picture is also interesting in that it provides clear evidence of the disparity between individual units of the LDV, (the soldier kneeling on the left, again proudly displaying his medal ribbons, is wearing an LDV armband), in the early days after its establishment. It is surprising to see a unit of the LDV so well equipped with uniforms, helmets, armoured-car (albeit improvised), machine-gun and even pistols, whilst others would have been lucky to have been able to muster a couple of pitch-forks and the odd wooden club!

One of the first standardised military production vehicles which was supplied to the Home Guard was the Beaverette. The story of the development of this vehicle really starts on the beaches of Dunkirk. In May 1940, following the capitulation of Belgium, the British government began to realise that the military situation in France was becoming hopeless. Churchill was forced to suggest that "as a precautionary measure, the Admiralty should assemble a large number of vessels in readiness to proceed to ports and inlets on the French Coast". Operation 'Dynamo' formally went into action at 18.57 hours on the 26th May 1940. The results were spectacular. By the 4th June, the amazing armada of more than 1,000 boats had recovered 113,000 French and 338,226 Allied soldiers in what has become known as the 'miracle of Dunkirk'. The evacuation led to one of the most pressing issues that faced this country for the whole war - a lack of equipment. In the retreat from France the British Expeditionary Force had been forced to leave behind all its equipment, representing much of the best that the British Army possessed. Expecting that a German invasion was imminent, no army vehicles could be spared for the defence of airfields or protection of factories. Lord Beaverbrook, the then minister of aircraft production, set about obtaining his own vehicles. The result was the Beaverette Mark I, (**below**), a design that was to be named after its benefactor. The chassis most commonly used was that of the 14hp passenger car produced by the Standard Motor Company LTD of Coventry, though the Humber Super Snipe was another source. Fitted to the car chassis was a body of mild steel to a maximum thickness of 0.35in. A layer of 3in thick oak planks bolted behind the steel reinforced the frontal armour. Both the Mark I and Mark II had an open roof, and were powered by an engine developing 45hp with a four-speed gearbox. Armament was provided by a Bren light machine-gun or, infrequently, a Boys anti-tank rifle. The Mark II could be distinguished from the Mark I by increased rear protection and horizontal as opposed to vertical radiator grills. The later Mark III had a fully enclosed fighting compartment with a small turret on top. Weighing in at 3 tons, it could only muster a top speed of 24mph! The end of the line was the Mark IV, which differed in the design of the hull top. The total production run of all four Marks ended with the completion of over 2,800 examples of the type.

To finish with are two illustrations of perhaps the most important vehicle within any military unit, Home Guard or otherwise - the tea wagon! The picture **above** shows an example that strictly speaking is not a form of transport, but which needs transporting itself. It is the tea caravan that served the 20th (Hailsham) Battalion, Sussex Home Guard. The example **below**, visibly well stocked, is more self-sufficient. Unfortunately from this picture one is unable to tell whether the lorry was a military or civilian type, though whatever the case it has been well painted in camouflage colours. The markings on the rear bodywork show that this is from another Sussex Home Guard unit - 'D' Company, 21st Sussex (Eastbourne) Battalion. Here some of the unit's men enjoy a break in manoeuvres whilst training on The Crumbles at Eastbourne.

www.historicmilitarypress.com.